It's the Gift That Keeps You Living

FORGIVE

By

Gwendolyn B. Elmore

Published by Truly In His Hands March 2021

TRULY IN HIS
HANDS
Your Family Does Matter - "Love Is What It Does"

ISBN-13: 978-0-9897328-4-0

PRINTED IN THE UNITED STATES OF AMERICA

I have dedicated this book to my darling, loving husband, Eugene, who has been a great supporter with his love, advice, and patience. I want to thank him for all that he has done to help me discover my strength in the ability to keep forgiving as commanded to. Thank you so much for the encouragement each day to keep moving forward.

I love you!!!

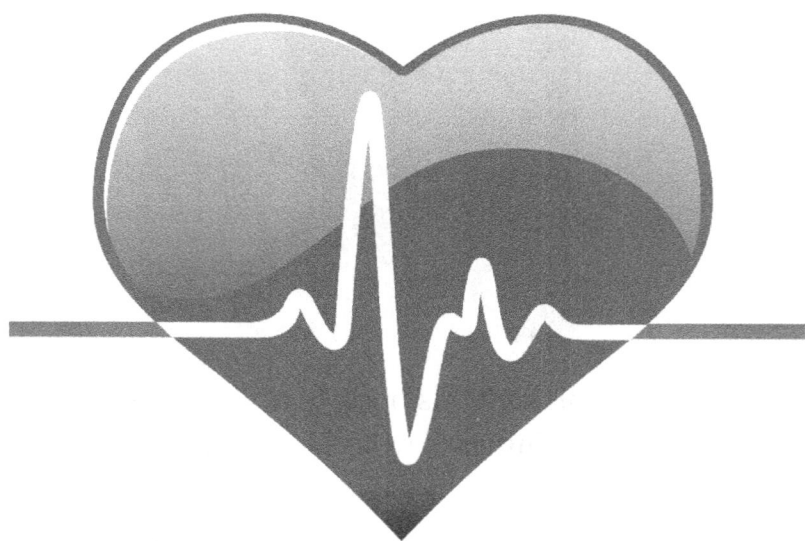

INTRODUCTION

In life things will happen, people will hurt us whether intentional or unintentional, but it is clearly up to us to walk in forgiveness towards others. We cannot always be responsible for how others treat us, but we can make the decision to forgive. Contrary to popular belief forgiving is a gift you give yourself. The other person may never suffer or the wrong done to you but if you do not forgive it will cost you. Throw away your idea that you will make them pay.

Some forgive and forget, more forgive, and remember, most forgive and remind. ~Robert B~

Be kind to each other, tenderhearted, forgiving one another,
just as God through Christ has forgiven you.

Ephesians 4:32 KJV

Be kind to one another, compassionate, forgiving each other,
just as God in Christ also has forgiven you.

Ephesians 4:32 NASB

And be ye kind one to another, having good bowels, favoring
each other, as also God in Christ Jesus favored you.

Ephesians 4:32 SLT Bible

CLEAR YOUR MIND
AND
FREE YOUR HEART

FORGIVE

Have you ever done anything that you needed forgiveness for? It is almost, nearly impossible not to have done something that required another's forgiveness. There is power in forgiveness. What does it really mean to forgive? When you forgive someone that has wronged you in some way, you release yourself from seeking revenge. So many people would rather have chance to say, "they hurt me, but I got them back" or "I bet they won't try me again". It may feel good at that moment and your ego has been stroked but, what happens afterwards?

Understanding what forgive means can help you understand in depth importance of forgiving not for the other person but more for yourself.

Wikipedia's definition of forgiveness is forgiveness, in a psychological sense, is the intentional and voluntary process by which one who may initially feel victimized, undergoes a change in feelings and attitude regarding a given offense, and overcomes negative emotions such as resentment and vengeance. Theorists differ, however, in the extent to which they believe forgiveness also implies replacing the negative emotions with positive attitudes. In certain legal contexts, forgiveness is a term for absolving or giving up all claims on account of debt, loan, obligation, or other claims.

Forgiveness is the act of pardoning an offender. In the Bible, the Greek word translated "forgiveness" literally means "to let go," as when a person does not demand payment for a debt. *Bible Dictionary*

One definition of forgive is to stop feeling angry or resentful toward (someone) for an offense, flaw, or mistake.

Another definition for forgive is it means to cancel (a debt)

Forgiveness is the act of pardoning an offender. In the Bible, the Greek word translated "forgiveness" literally means "to let go," as when a person does not demand payment for a debt.

While everyone is into credit repair, we should encourage each other to cancel the debt. Forgive others and let it go. Do you like it when something appears on your credit that you know should have been removed? Well that feeling is how we treat others when we keep bringing up their past offenses towards you. Wipe the slate clean, you have the power now to make a difference and have your sins forgiven. FORGIVE AND LET IT GO

And when you stand praying, if you hold anything against anyone, forgive them, so that your father in heaven may forgive you your sins. Mark 11:25 KJV

Whenever you stand praying, if you have anything against anyone, forgive him [drop the issue, let it go], so that your

Father who is in heaven will also forgive you your
transgressions and wrongdoings [against Him and others].

Mark 11:25 AMP

And whenever you stand praying, if you have anything against
anyone, forgive him and let it drop (leave it, let it go), in order
that your Father Who is in heaven may also forgive you your
[own] failings and shortcomings and let them drop.

Mark 11:25 AMPC

And when ye stand praying, forgive, if ye have ought against
any: that your Father also which is in heaven may forgive you
your trespasses.

Mark 11:25 BRG

And whenever you stand praying, if you have anything against
anyone, forgive him, so that your Father in heaven will also
forgive you your wrongdoing."

Mark 11:25 CSB

And whenever you stand up to pray, if you have something
against anyone, forgive so that your Father in heaven may
forgive you your wrongdoings."

Mark 11:25 CEB

And when you stand praying, if you have anything against anyone, forgive him; so that your Father in heaven may also forgive your offenses."

"Do not repay evil for evil or reviling for reviling, but on the contrary, bless, for to this you were called, that you may obtain a blessing.

1 Peter 3:9

"Let all bitterness and wrath and anger and clamor and slander be put away from you, along with all malice.

Ephesians 4:31 KJV

"But if you do not forgive others their sins, your father will not forgive your sins."

Matthew 6:15 KJV

With these scriptures in mind and you wanting answered prayers why would not you want to forgive? When you think about it so much is on the line that affects not only you, but those whom you love so dearly. Your prayers unheard is not a chance you want to take. Just think for a moment….what things have you been praying for? Maybe peace in your family, restoration of relationship with an estranged loved one, you may need a physical healing, to conceive a baby, that pay raise, the dream home, the straying spouse, the wayward child, or the family business. To know that you have one thing that maybe just an act of forgiveness away.

Our parents raised nine children and one of the life lessons they taught us was to love and forgive others. They never allowed us to remain upset with each other, we had to stand before them and make it right. The lesson to be learned is that if you learn to forgive those whom you live with everyday then you will not have a hard time forgiving those who live outside the home. We were not allowed to go to bed angry. It was not something that was an option, we just had to do it. After all The Word of God clearly states for us not to let the sun go down on our wrath.

Be ye angry , and sin not: let not the sun go down upon your wrath: neither give place to the devil.

Ephesians 4:25-26 KJV

Give the gift to yourself. Forgiveness, the very word forgive comes from the root word, give. Forgiveness releases you, the offended from being in a prison by our negative thoughts and judgments. It takes the poison out of our bodies and cleanses our system of the poison that will surely fester and cause illness. We cannot take the poison and expect someone else to die. The ones we cannot seem to forgive go on with their lives and we are ones left suffering if we do not choose to forgive.

"Forgive people their trespasses [their reckless and willful sins, leaving them, letting them go, and giving up resentment], your heavenly Father will also forgive you" Amplified Bible Matthew 6:14-15

The following pages contains
provided by The Mayo Clinic has
granted with permission to use, with
the agreement that their content
remains the same.

Forgiveness: Letting go of grudges and bitterness

When someone you care about hurts you, you can hold on to anger, resentment and thoughts of revenge — or embrace forgiveness and move forward.

By Mayo Clinic staff

Nearly everyone has been hurt by the actions or words of another. Perhaps your mother criticized your parenting skills, your colleague sabotaged a project, or your partner had an affair. These wounds can leave you with lasting feelings of anger, bitterness or even vengeance — but if you don't practice forgiveness, you might be the one who pays most dearly. By embracing forgiveness, you can also embrace peace, hope, gratitude, and joy. Consider how forgiveness can lead you down the path of physical, emotional and spiritual well-being.

What is forgiveness?

Generally, forgiveness is a decision to let go of resentment and thoughts of revenge. The act that hurt or offended you might always remain a part of your life, but forgiveness can lessen its grip on you and help you focus on other, positive parts of your life. Forgiveness can even lead to feelings of understanding, empathy and compassion for the one who hurt you.

Forgiveness doesn't mean that you deny the other person's responsibility for hurting you, and it doesn't minimize or justify the wrong. You can forgive the person without excusing the act. Forgiveness brings a kind of peace that helps you go on with life.

What are the benefits of forgiving someone?

Letting go of grudges and bitterness can make way for compassion, kindness and peace. Forgiveness can lead to:

- Healthier relationships
- Greater spiritual and psychological well-being
- Less anxiety, stress and hostility
- Lower blood pressure
- Fewer symptoms of depression
- Lower risk of alcohol and substance abuse

Why is it so easy to hold a grudge?

When you're hurt by someone you love and trust, you might become angry, sad or confused. If you dwell on hurtful events or situations, grudges filled with resentment, vengeance and hostility can take root. If you allow negative feelings to crowd out positive feelings, you might find yourself swallowed up by your own bitterness or sense of injustice.

What are the effects of holding a grudge?

If you're unforgiving, you might pay the price repeatedly by bringing anger and bitterness into every relationship and new experience. Your life might become so wrapped up in the wrong that you can't enjoy the present. You might become depressed or anxious. You might feel that your life lacks meaning or purpose, or that you're at odds with your spiritual beliefs. You might lose valuable and enriching connectedness with others.

How do I reach a state of forgiveness?

Forgiveness is a commitment to a process of change. To begin, you might:

- Consider the value of forgiveness and its importance in your life at a given time
- Reflect on the facts of the situation, how you've reacted, and how this combination has affected your life, health and well-being
- When you're ready, actively choose to forgive the person who's offended you
- Move away from your role as victim and release the control and power the offending person and situation have had in your life

As you let go of grudges, you'll no longer define your life by how you've been hurt. You might even find compassion and understanding.

FORGIVENESS: LETTING GO OF GRUDGES AND BITTERNESS
WHAT HAPPENS IF I CAN'T FORGIVE SOMEONE?

Forgiveness can be challenging, especially if the person who's hurt you doesn't admit wrong or doesn't speak of his or her sorrow. If you find yourself stuck, consider the situation from the other person's point of view. Ask yourself why he or she would behave in such a way. Perhaps you would have reacted similarly if you faced the same situation. In addition, consider broadening your view of the world. Expect occasional imperfections from the people in your life. You might want to reflect on times you've hurt others and on those who've forgiven you. It can also be helpful to write in a journal, pray or use guided meditation — or talk with a person you've found to be wise and compassionate, such as a spiritual leader, a mental health provider, or an impartial loved one or friend.

DOES FORGIVENESS GUARANTEE RECONCILIATION?

If the hurtful event involved someone whose relationship you otherwise value, forgiveness can lead to reconciliation. This isn't always the case, however. Reconciliation might be impossible if the offender has died or is unwilling to communicate with you. In other cases, reconciliation might not be appropriate. Still, forgiveness is possible — even if reconciliation isn't.

WHAT IF I HAVE TO INTERACT WITH THE PERSON WHO HURT ME BUT I DON'T WANT TO?

If you haven't reached a state of forgiveness, being near the person who hurt you might be tense and stressful. To handle these situations, remember that you can choose to attend or avoid specific functions and gatherings. Respect yourself and do what seems best. If you choose to attend, don't be surprised by a certain amount of awkwardness and perhaps even more intense feelings. Do your best to keep an open heart and mind. You might find that the experience helps you to move forward with forgiveness.

WHAT IF THE PERSON I'M FORGIVING DOESN'T CHANGE?

Getting another person to change his or her actions, behavior or words isn't the point of forgiveness. Think of forgiveness more about how it can change your life — by bringing you peace, happiness, and emotional and spiritual healing. Forgiveness can take away the power the other person continues to wield in your life.

WHAT IF I'M THE ONE WHO NEEDS FORGIVENESS?

The first step is to honestly assess and acknowledge the wrongs you've done and how those wrongs have affected others. At the same time, avoid judging yourself too harshly. You're human, and you'll make mistakes. If you're truly sorry for something you've said or done, consider admitting it to those you've harmed. Speak of your sincere sorrow or regret, and specifically ask for forgiveness — without making excuses. Remember, however, you can't force someone to forgive you. Others need to move to forgiveness in their own time. Whatever the outcome, commit to treating others with compassion, empathy and respect.

Used by permission. The Mayo Clinic gave permission to publish this information in the book, exactly the way it was published. I was not to make any changes and I did just that.

THE MAYO CLINIC ENDS HERE

Has reading this book up to this point did you think of any person that you feel like you need to forgive and release the hurt? This a good time to just stop and think about it, pray for wisdom on how to deal with the unforgiveness in your heart right now. You may be just discovering that it was there. Sit quiet for about 5 minutes and if after those 5 minutes you discover that there is someone, now you need to say this prayer:

Father, I choose to forgive (name each person that came to mind while you have been reading this book) Your Word says that if I do not forgive others their trespasses you will not forgive my trespasses. I do not ever want to be in a position of needing your forgiveness and not being able to receive it. I ask Holy Spirit to guide me in my decisions I make in allowing to be easily offended by what others say or do to me. Help me to quickly recognize when that has happened so I can correct it immediately. Amein

After praying this prayer, do not think there will not be any opposition to what you just prayed. The key to victorious overcomes is remember this one thing, holding something in your heart for an offense delays your forgiveness from who you need it from the most. Make quick adjustments and keep it moving. You always want your days to be filled with the Peace of God and your mind to be free of the thoughts of the offense.

How much more, then, will the blood of Christ, who through the eternal Spirit offered himself unblemished to God, cleanse our consciences from acts that lead to death, so that we may serve the living God!

Hebrews 9:14 NIV

Just think how much more the blood of Christ will purify our consciences from sinful deeds[a] so that we can worship the living God. For by the power of the eternal Spirit, Christ offered himself to God as a perfect sacrifice for our sins.

Hebrews 9:14 NLT

how much more will the blood of Christ, who through the eternal [Holy] Spirit willingly offered Himself unblemished [that is, without moral or spiritual imperfection as a sacrifice] to God, cleanse your conscience from dead works and lifeless observances to serve the ever living God?

Hebrews 9:14 AMP

Let this scripture be part of your process to overcome thoughts that are dead works and contrary to obeying the instructions given in the Bible. Sometimes we allow thoughts of wrongdoings of others to take up space in our minds without considering how those thoughts are affecting us. Our bodies began to feel those affects and now our bodies respond in such a way that now our health is now. While studies have proven that some diseases come for the food supply, the water some drink and the air we breathe. Many diseases start from holding on to unforgiveness. Please do more research should on your own so that you so not fall victim to any of these diseases.

Finally, believers, whatever is true, whatever is honorable and worthy of respect, whatever is right and confirmed by God's word, whatever is pure and wholesome, whatever is lovely and brings peace, whatever is admirable and of good repute; if there is any excellence, if there is anything worthy of praise, think continually on these things [center your mind on them, and implant them in your heart].

Philippians 4:8 AMP

For the rest, brethren, whatever is true, whatever is worthy of reverence and is honorable and seemly, whatever is just, whatever is pure, whatever is lovely and lovable, whatever is kind and winsome and gracious, if there is any virtue and excellence, if there is anything worthy of praise, think on and weigh and take account of these things [fix your minds on them]. Philippians 4:8 AMPC

Finally, brethren, whatsoever things are true, whatsoever things are honest, whatsoever things are just, whatsoever things are pure, whatsoever things are lovely, whatsoever things are of good report; if there be any virtue, and if there be any praise, think on these things.

Philippians 4:8 CRB

Finally brothers and sisters, whatever is true, whatever is honorable, whatever is just, whatever is pure, whatever is lovely, whatever is commendable—if there is any moral excellence and if there is anything praiseworthy—dwell on these things.

Philippians 4:8 CSB

From now on, brothers and sisters, if anything is excellent and if anything is admirable, focus your thoughts on these things: all that is true, all that is holy, all that is just, all that is pure, all that is lovely, and all that is worthy of praise.

Philippians 4:8 CEB

Philippians 4:8 tells us what things we should be always keeping on our minds. It is clear that things these aren't of moral excellence and praiseworthy, we should not think about. Just a moment think, is keeping the negative feeling of hurt and pain listed there? Certainly not! And there is good reason for that. Does it feel good to think about it? What kind of feelings come up? Not any that are praiseworthy. Unguarded thoughts can take your heart to a place that will cause you to react in a way you should not.

We have to purposely be kind and loving toward one another, especially at home. One major problem that we have with loving others is how we think about them (mind), which causes us to feel a certain way (emotions), and then we choose to act a certain way towards them (will). Our mind is our thinker, our emotions are our feeler, and our will is our chooser. Whenever we think, we begin to feel a certain way, and then we choose to respond, or not respond, a certain way. Again Philippians 4:8 instructs us to focus our minds on lovely thoughts, things that are pure, things that are just.

Why should we forgive? The most important reason we should is because as born-again believers it is something that God has said for us to do. When we do not, we hinder our prayers from being answered.

So often we think we are doing the person a favor by forgiving them, but we are giving ourselves the greatest gift for us. The power to forgive allows us to free ourselves from the anger and the pain of the act that was committed against us.

There are many things that will require your forgiveness. Infidelity, lies, harsh words, stealing etc., in many instances the pain is still there. We cannot say how deep the pain should be because everyone experiences hurt and pain differently.

Did you know that if we would just use the Word of God as a true guide daily, we could prevent or lessen many of the health challenges we face? Our eyes and ears should be guard daily and often during the day. These are gateways to our spirit.

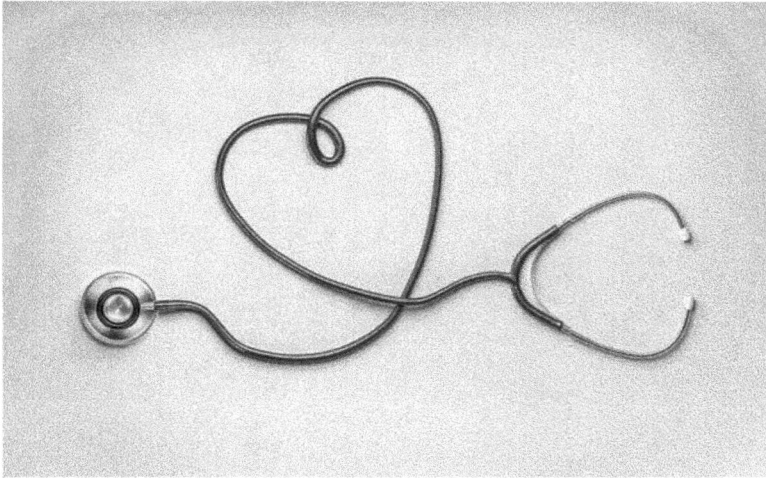

Protect your Health

Heart

Mind

Forgive So
You Can
Live

FREE YOUR MIND
AND
CLEAR YOUR HEART

1. ADMIT YOU ARE OFFENDED
2. PRAY TO ASK FOR HELP
3. CHOOSE TO FORGIVE
4. RELEASE THE OFFENDER
5. STOP REHEARSING IT
6. LET IT GO

FORGIVING OTHERS IS A CHOICE YOU MAKE , THE DECISION IS TOTALLY UP TO YOU, BUT IF I WERE YOU ,I WOULD MAKE THE CHOICE TO FORGIVE.

STORY TIME

This story is based on real life experiences and events. It is my hope that these stories will give you an actual account of the things that can happen when you make the choice to forgive or not to forgive.

This story about real life events of The Late Intercessor Willerma Frazier Riley, she was the oldest and first born of Dr. Patrick and Minister Cora Lee Cohen Frazier. With her given permission and consent before she passed away on May 18, 2016. When she knew this book would be written on forgiveness, she wanted me to make sure to include her story so others can realize just how unforgiveness can affect your health and the lives of those who love and care about you.

Willerma, was a loving caring person and would give her last to help others in need. She had such an ability to get others involved in being a blessing to others. It was such a joy to watch her do one of the things she enjoyed.

Willerma was a prayer intercessor, a prayer warrior and no matter what she was going through she never waivered in praying for those who needed prayer. She was known to pray at the drop of a dime. If you called her for prayer, she was praying right then.

There are so many wonderful things that could be said about her, because she was so incredibly special to so many people.

Her love is felt by so many lives that she touched while she was on this earth. No one can ever replace her, she was "one of a kind".

Let us start this story off at the onset of the diagnosis of the disease called, breast cancer.

In 2007, Willerma got a report from a mammogram. The report came back abnormal, there was tumor in her breast. What was she to do? One thing she was not going to do at that time was radiation or chemotherapy, she was totally against both. The horror stories and the information she had read was that both destroyed the good cells too. I guess you all are probably wondering what she did. This was her decision, and she chose to trust God and believe for her healing.

Everyone that loved her was concerned, most just wanted her to do what the doctors recommended so she could have a chance to live longer. The options given weren't any that she would choose, and for the next 7 years she did nothing but prayed about and trusted that she would experience healing also. And why wouldn't she? She has seen our father survive melanoma for 18 years without any radiation or chemotherapy. Surely this is the right route for her to take. He trusted God and she saw him stand on the Word of God on healing.

Fast forward 7 years, a scan showed that the tumor had not increased in size in those years, that was a miracle. No one could have prepared her and any who loved her for what was about to happen. Willerma decided to have another opinion for removing the tumor from her breast so in April 2015 she had another doctor examine her to get his opinion. Now at that time, there was evidence before he went in, that a biopsy was already done and it had been tagged. There was also what looked like a water puddle that surrounded the tumor, that seem to be protecting it. When the doctor went in he ruptured that protection that was there and of course the cancer began to spread rapidly. This was the beginning of her discovering the spiritual side of what was happening.

Willerma had prayed for so many over the years and testimony of healings given time and time again. Surely, she would have the same testimony. This began a journey of finding the right solution to the problem. What do you do when your prayers for yourself does not seem to be working? What happens when your healing is not instantly? How do you continue to pray for others, watch them get healed and you are desiring to have the same testimony? Willerma continued to have her 5:00 a.m. Prayer Call like she had done for many years. Just because she was going through a health crisis, did not mean she could just drop it, she still got up and prayed for others.

Willerma did not take well to having radiation and chemotherapy so she sought to find a holistic way of healing. She tried several means of trying to get cured through all-natural means. She reached to a doctor in California who in their very first conversation revealed to her that her breast cancer had spiritual reason behind it. He told her that she was hurt by a male and had not totally forgiven him. What? Surely, she had forgiven everyone and any that had hurt or offended her. What was he implying? Willerma called me and told me of the conversation she had with the doctor. She was trying to figure out who the man was she had not forgiven. Our talk led to me telling her she had not forgiven her ex-husband. She said that she had and that was not possible.

That night, when she went to sleep, she had a dream about her ex-husband was in a room at a gathering and he kept trying to get close to her as if he wanted to have a conversation with her. Each time he got closer she would go another way to avoid any contact with him. When she called the next morning to discuss the dream with me, I told her that was the man you had not really forgiven. Willerma said she had but the more we talked and the more we went into details about her marriage to her ex-husband it became apparent to her that she had not completely forgiven him.

It is her desire that every person reading this story will search their hearts to see if there is any unforgiveness in their hearts that they are not aware of. To help you, the reader to understand the importance of letting go of the hurt and pain you experience because is vital to your health.

A Brief Insight of her first marriage

Never in Willerma's life did she think she would get married, and it would end in divorce and not until death do us part. based on the understanding of The Word of God. Marriage was to continue until death due you part. Her understanding of the scriptures and church affiliation believed that if you get married and divorce you could not get married again. A person could only get remarried if the spouse died. So can you imagine being married for 22 years and your spouse decides that he is not happy, and he leaves, while you are a leader in your denomination that he had been present with you to the all the church conferences, he had driven you to the churches you pastored for many years. Everyone knew him in our small community. He had become a friend to many, had been a part of every part of her life and now he wanted to leave? This was not easy for her, what would she do, how would she explain this to her family, her church, her community who he had woven himself in and not to mention to her members she was pastoring at the time.

Because of the upbringing the only way she could remarry was if he died. How many of you know that because of what her upbringing and understanding of the scriptures, death would be better than divorce? Well, it was not death that ended the marriage it was divorce. Okay now the battle in her mind with continuing to be a pastor. How would she continue to lead God's people? This was a struggle in mind even though she kept serving as a pastor. As time went on, she thought she had forgiven her ex-husband completely.

Without going into every detail let us fast forward 22 years later when she finds out that she had not completely forgiven her ex-husband. The doctor from California told her that a male hurt her and had not forgiven him. Now she was remarried to a wonderful Man of God who did not think a second thought about doing everything he could to make sure that she would receive healing. So, when she discusses the dream with Floyd and what we had discussed, he immediately told her to find out where he was, and he would drive her to take her there so her healing would be complete.

The day came when she would meet face to face her ex-husband of 22 years whom she had been divorced from for 22 years. You can only imagine the emotions that she begins to experience as they took the two- and half-hour drive. What would she say? How would her coming be received? He was remarried now and had been for several years. Floyd was very encouraging, he wanted her to have this behind her so they could enjoy life together beyond the battle with cancer. He wanted her to be able to enjoy the life that God has blessed them with together at this time. By the way, Floyd and Willerma were just recently married at this time.

Well, they finally got there. Floyd being the gentlemen he was and is, got out and went to the door. His recap of what happened when the door opened, he did not recognize the ex-husband. He knew him well, but the person that stood at the door frail and fragile, so he asked for him by name. When the man that opened the door said he was who Floyd was looking for, he was almost speechless. He explained, he was now Willerma's husband and the reason why he was there. Willerma was in the car and needed to talk with him. Well, there was no turning back now she was here and now she would be face to face with the person who she thought she had forgiven but it was clear that was not the case.

The face-to-face meeting was not really what she expected. To see her ex-husband, who had been verbally abusive to her for years looking more than 30 years his age, was a shock. All she could feel for him was compassion. Life had not treated him well and his health was failing. Without giving a verbatim account of the conversation, let us proceed to the forgiveness part. Willerma told her ex-husband she was the to let hm know that she has forgiven him, and she asked his forgiveness. Her ex-husband told her that back a few months ago he had started to make a trip to see her to ask her forgiveness for the way he treated her during their marriage, and he wanted her to forgive him. WOW….the power of God is TRULY AMAZING. They both were at the same place in their lives concerning forgiveness. After that visit now came the process of beginning to heal. How many of you know that was also a continuing process? As time went on, she knew within herself that she finally had the peace that she had released that pain and forgiveness that healing from the offense had taken place.

Willerma continued to focus on the health challenge that she had been facing. Soon she would learn that her ex-husband passed away, just a few months after going to visit him. How she knew she had completely forgiven him; she was now concerned about if he got a proper burial. He was ex-military and she wanted to make sure that her ex-husband was given that honor. She asked Floyd if he would take her to the gravesite and so he agreed to do that for her.

Why did she want this story shared? She wanted others to understand how important it is to make sure you take the necessary steps to completely heal after being hurt or have experienced an offense. One could have all the titles before and after their names but what offenses are they taking around with them in their hearts? No one can see what is actually in out hearts but our Creator, our Maker, our Father who is The Most High.

It was her desire that everyone reading her story would take inventory of their heart and see what is in it against others because they hurt you. One of enemy's tactics he uses has not changed, the spirit of offense. Why? Because he wants you to stay in broken fellowship and communication with our Creator, our Father, The Most High.

Is Infidelity Forgivable?

Does forgiveness have choices? What is meant by that statement is, do we have a choice on deciding what we will or will not forgive? So often we think we can pick and choose which actions are forgivable towards us. The Bible makes it truly clear on how we are to forgive others for the wrong done to us.

While the pain of adultery often leads to divorce, it does not have to. Making decision to forgive your spouse and work on developing your relationship with the Holy Spirit is vital so that offense does not happen again. Everyone handles hurt differently and this is not to minimize anyone's feeling. Can a spouse forgive the other spouse for cheating? Can the marriage restoration occur? Can a spouse trust again? These are questions that come to mind. Well, the answers to these questions are yes. It is possible to have an even better marriage afterwards.

[But] whoso committeth adultery with a woman lacketh understanding: he [that] doeth it destroyeth his own soul.

Proverbs 6:32

- But I say unto you, That whosoever looketh on a woman to lust after her hath committed adultery with her already in his heart.

Matthew 5:28

The first step for the cheating spouse to admit it, not only for the other spouse but for themselves. Admitting that they messed up helps them hear themselves say what they did. The second step, do not make excuses for why you did it based on your unhappiness with your spouse. The thing about cheating is that it is a selfish decision one makes to satisfy themselves. Why selfish? Who in the marriage benefited from the act? What did it do for your spouse and your marriage? The work selfish simply means **concerned excessively or exclusively with oneself** : seeking or concentrating on one's own advantage, pleasure, or well-being without regard for others. Anyone who tells you they cheated to better their marriage is a liar. If that was the truth than why wasn't it discussed with your spouse before you did it? And why would it be a problem now after it was revealed? The cheating spouse and the person they cheated with were the only two that benefited from the act?

. For he that soweth of his flesh shall of the flesh reap corruption; but he that soweth to the Spirit shall of the Spirit reap life everlasting.

Galatians 6:8 King James Version

Do not be deceived. You cannot fool God. A man will get back whatever he plants! If a man does things to please his sinful old self, his soul will be lost. If a man does things to please the Holy Spirit, he will have life that lasts forever

Galatians 6:7-8 New Life Version

Cheating is not meant to satisfy both spouses, not even, not ever. It one means of the enemy's attempt to destroy the family. Not to give him credit but to have you not ignorant of the devices he uses. Sin is pleasurable for a moment but often the consequences outweigh the pleasure. Those moments of pleasure take you out of the presence of The Creator, The Most High, our Father. Your relationship suffers and broken fellowship with Him and now that person has separated from Him as all sin does. That is a huge price to pay.

Adultery is wrong for all God's people. If you possess the name Of Christ, if you have been washed in the Blood of The Lamb and you commit adultery, you have given an invitation for some chaos to directly affect your family. One of the things that happens is, sometimes everyone else knows before your family does.

Just imagine, you are in a position of leadership now you have not only hurt your wife and children but now the people you are serving. WOW....so you see sin not only affects your house but God's people too. The people who look up to you for spiritual guidance now question your decisions. If the leader can fall then what hope is there for those struggling with weaknesses. While their hope is the Lord, we know that sometime the only Bible people read is the life they see leaders living. It is human nature for people to not sit in judgement but expect that those that are leading them to have matured and grown spiritually beyond the point of falling into fleshy sin.

There are some people that believe what The Word of God says concerning those in leadership such as pastors, ministers, elders, deacons and anyone that has been chosen to lead members in any leadership position. None of us are exempt from following The Word of God. Spiritual leaders are called are called to a higher standard of living according to Titus 1:6, 7 and 1 Timothy 3:2-7.

Here's what you should look for in an elder: he should be above suspicion; *if he is married, he should* be the husband of one wife, raise children who believe, and be a person who can't be accused of rough and raucous living. It is necessary that any overseer *you appoint* be blameless, as he is entrusted with God's mission. *Look for someone who* isn't pompous or quick to anger, who is not a drunkard, violent, or chasing after seedy gain *or worldly fame.*
Titus 1:6-7 The Voice Bible

if a man is blameless, the husband of one wife, having faithful children not accused of dissipation or insubordination. For a bishop must be blameless, as a steward of God, not self-willed, not quick-tempered, not given to wine, not violent, not greedy for money,
Titus:1-6 New King James Version

Some may say well they are human too; they make mistakes too. While this is true every scripture written in the Bible with our best interest in mind. We can choose to do right or wrong. When we make The Word of God, THE FINAL AUTHORITY, our choice should be one that pleases; Him.

A church leader should be above reproach devoted to his wife, her being the only woman. Not this new age trend that he can have a chic on the side in town and out of town if no one else knows. Husbands are to love their wives as Christ loved the church. They are love them only with their mind, will and their emotions, not just for sex.

But whoso committeth adultery with a woman lacketh understanding: he that doeth it destroyeth his own soul.
Proverbs 6:32

What happens when the sin has affected the ministry? Let us not attempt to say out of feelings but how The Bible tells us to handle it. You are probably saying you mean to tell me that there is an answer for even that in The Bible. Yes there is, but it is only used by those who really have reverence for The Creator and His Word. There are several scripture references on how to deal with an act of sin.

But now I have written to you not to keep company with anyone named a brother, who is sexually immoral, or covetous, or an idolater, or a reviler, or a drunkard, or an extortioner—not even to eat with such a person.

I Corinthians 5:11

Some may say why is adultery seems to be the worse sin that is committed. While sin maybe sin and they all carry the same penalty. The payment for all sin is death which breaks our fellowship with the Father who is our Creator. Adultery breaks fellowship with our spouse whom we entered into covenant with them and our Creator. It is one of the sexual sins that a person commits against their own body.

Flee from sexual immorality. Every other sin a person commits is outside the body, but the sexually immoral person sins against his own body.

I Corinthians 6:18

Now the Bible clearly tells us how to handle adultery in His House. There are instructions given in The Bible on handling a person who not only sins but does so repeatedly. Often the repeat offenders have no remorse on what they have done and nor the hurt and pain they have caused others.

"If your brother or sister sins, go and point out their fault, just between the two of you. If they listen to you, you have won them over. But if they will not listen, take one or two others along, so that every matter may be established by the testimony of two or three witnesses. If they still refuse to listen, tell it to the church; and if they refuse to listen even to the church, treat them as you would a pagan or a tax collector. Truly I tell you, whatever you bind on earth will be bound in heaven, and whatever you loose on earth will be loosed in heaven". Romans 18:15-18

Because God commands us to forgive the person who has hurt us and the sin of adultery must be forgiven by the spouse and others who it has affected. There are steps of healing that need to take place and the offender must not return to repeat the act. Do not cover up your sin and make excuses on why you did it. Take time to focus on why you should not do it again. Do not allow arrogance to settle in and make it about you. Do not play the blame game either. Your spouse is not the problem, you are the problem and dealing with it in a positive way is what you need to do. Admit the wrong and quit it. Seek Godly wisdom from someone who is trustworthy and is not going to side with your sin. One thing for sure about the loving God we serve He will talk to you first about and when you refuse to change, you get exposed. Exposure can destroy your family.

As much as we would like to sometimes, remember we cannot change what has been established in The Word of God. It is so simply to just follow the Basic Daily Instructions for Living on Earth. When we make up our minds to do that, our lives will be better.

This Book of the Law shall not depart from your mouth, but you shall read [and meditate on] it day and night, so that you may be careful to do [everything] in accordance with all that is written in it; for then you will make your way prosperous, and then you will be successful.

Joshua 1:8 AMP

This Book of the Law shall not depart out of your mouth, but you shall meditate on it day and night, that you may observe and do according to all that is written in it. For then you shall make your way prosperous, and then you shall deal wisely and have good success.

Joshua 1:8 AMPC

This book of instruction must not depart from your mouth; you are to meditate on it day and night so that you may carefully observe everything written in it. For then you will prosper and succeed in whatever you do.

Joshua 1:8 CSB

Never stop speaking about this Instruction scroll. Recite it day and night so you can carefully obey everything written in it. Then you will accomplish your objectives and you will succeed.

Joshua 1:8 CEB

Yes, keep this book of the Torah on your lips, and meditate on it day and night, so that you will take care to act according to everything written in it. Then your undertakings will prosper, and you will succeed.

Joshua 1:8 CJB

Long ago I promised the ancestors of Israel that I would give this land to their descendants. So be strong and brave! Be careful to do everything my servant Moses taught you. Never stop reading The Book of the Law he gave you. Day and night you must think about what it says. If you obey it completely, you and Israel will be able to take this land.

Joshua 1:8 CEV

This book of the law shall not depart from thy mouth; and thou shalt meditate upon it day and night, that thou mayest take heed to do according to all that is written therein; for then shalt thou have good success in thy ways, and then shalt thou prosper.

Joshua 1:8 DARBY

Let not the book of this law depart from thy mouth: but thou shalt meditate on it day and night, that thou mayst observe and do all things that are written in it: then shalt thou direct thy way, and understand it.

Joshua 1:8 DRA

Always remember what is written in that book of law. Speak about that book and study it day and night. Then you can be sure to obey what is written there. If you do this, you will be wise and successful in everything you do.

Joshua 1:8 ERV

This Book of the Law must never depart from your mouth, and you are to meditate on it day and night, so that you will act faithfully according to everything written in it, because then you will prosper in everything you do, and you will succeed.
Joshua 1:8 EHV

If we would take the time daily to meditate on Joshua 1:8 and the scriptures that deal with your current situation (sickness, anxiety, bitterness, wrath, and unforgiveness just to name a few) we will have the strength to forgive others.

Many spouses find it hard to forgive after the other spouse has broken their vows, but we are to forgive because The Father, our

42

Creator, our Maker, The Almighty God says so. The most common question is how could you do this to me? But is it all about what they did to you or others finding out what they cheated? Funny thing about that is, by the time the innocent spouse finds others already know. How many times have you disappointed the One who gives us life?

Can you get over the offense and past the pain? It is possible for you to move on, and your marriage become a Marriage By God's design. So often people give into the feelings of embarrassment, and others knowing but it is okay. You being embarrassed maybe because you had already been telling folks what you would not stand for in your marriage, that that would be the deal breaker. But how many are dealing with it for years and had no clue? You cannot change what has happened, The thing you say you will never do is the thing you end up doing. You must forgive and move forward. Know the plans that our Creator, our Father has for you. To do you good and not evil. Learn to give the same forgiveness He gives to you, now you give to others.

Forgive the person they committed the act with also, often the spirit of manipulation is being used to coerced them into it. Sometimes the offender fines someone who is weak minded and needy, and the person doesn't even know they are being played like a fiddle for the offender's own gratification. It happens so often, the vulnerability of people, male and females, can be spotted or sniffed out. Well, that is another book.

Yes, it hurts when the one you gave your heart to hurts you by breaking the marriage vows. The covenant was made between You and them and God. You think you are the only one hurting, grieving the pain? The Bible commands us to forgive them. It takes meditation of The Word of God daily to overcome the pain, but it can be done.

One of our former presidents said this about Nelson Mandela:

"Mandela made a grand, elegant, dignified exit from prison and it was enormously powerful for the world to see. But as I watched him walking down that dusty road, I wondered whether he was thinking about the last 27 years, whether he was angry all over again. Later, many years later, I had a chance to ask him. I said, 'Come on, you were a great man, you invited your jailers to your inauguration, you put your pressures on the government. But tell me the truth. Weren't you really angry all over again?' And he said, 'Yes, I was angry. And I was a little afraid. After all I have not been free in so long. But he said, 'when I felt that anger well up inside of me, I realized that if I hated them after I got outside that gate then they would still have me.' And he smiled and said, 'I wanted to be free, so I let it go.' It was an astonishing moment in my life. It changed me."

ABOUT THE AUTHOR

GWENDOLYN B. ELMORE is a wife, a mother, a friend, a singer/songwriter, an author, Certified Marriage Educator/Coach and Certified Marriage Mentor.

She is married to Eugene Elmore, an anointed man of God. They have three adult children, Terrance Patrick (Nicole), Trenise Genyetta and Jeffrey Bernard (Brittany). She is the doting grandmother of Michelle Renae, Jeremiah Patrick, Payse Frazier, Olivia Patrice and Jacob Jeffrey.

She believes that forgiveness is the key to true success in life. She also believes that hugs are important to one's health.

Follow The Marriage Educator Coach on Social Media.

WordPress Blog: http://medicministry.blog

Facebook: https://www.facebook.com/medicministry

Instagram: @themarriageeducatorcoach